Disabilities and Differences

We All Learn

Revised Edition

Rebecca Rissman

capstone

To Contact Capstone Global Library,
please call 800-747-4992, or visit our website www.mycapstone.com

Printed in the United States of America.
009926R

Library of Congress Cataloging-in-Publication Data is available on the Library of Congress website.
978-1-4846-3626-8 (revised paperback)
978-1-4846-3655-8 (ebook)

Image Credits
age fotostock: Banana Stock, 14, It Stock Free, 9; Getty Images: BRIAN MITCHELL, 10, Jack Hollingsworth, 4, ullstein bild, 15; iStockphoto: amlanmathur, 11, Christopher Futcher, 16, 23 Bottom; Shutterstock: Alsu, 23 Top, karelnoppe, 6, 23 Middle, Monkey Business Images, Cover, 12, 13, 19, 21, 22, Phovoir, 7, Rawpixel.com, 18, wavebreakmedia, Cover Back, 8, 17, 20

Contents

Differences

We are all different.

Learning

We learn facts.

We learn skills.

We learn to swim.

We learn to read.

How We Learn

People learn in different ways.

People learn in different places.

Some people learn by listening.

Some people learn by seeing.

Some people learn by moving.

Braille

Some people learn by sitting.

Some people learn by touching.

Some people learn by writing.

Some people learn alone.

Some people learn in groups.

Where We Learn

We can learn at home.

We can learn at school.

We Are All Different

We all learn in different ways.
How do you learn?

Words to Know

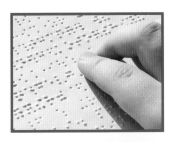 **Braille** raised bumps on paper. People read Braille with their fingers.

 **computer** machine that can help some students communicate, read, and write

 **teacher's aid** person who gives students extra help

This section includes related vocabulary words that can help students learn about this topic. Use these words to explore learning.

Index

Note to Parents and Teachers

Before reading

Ask children to form pairs and find three ways in which they are different, for example height, hair color, eyes, or clothes. Then explain that although they are all unique they also have things in common. Talk to the children about the different ways we learn. Ask them how they think they learn to walk, talk, read, and write. Explain that people learn in different ways and that different skills require different ways of learning.

After reading

Ask the children to work with a partner and to think of three different ways they learn (listening, reading, being shown what to do, or working alone). Collect their answers and make a chart on the board for the students to see. Explain that there are many ways to learn.